FUN WITH THE BANJO

by Mel Bay

This book was created to help you have fun with the *banjo*. It will provide enjoyment and satisfaction to anyone desiring to play — so pick up your *banjo* and *have fun!*

Audio Contents

Audio
www.melbay.com/93268EB

Video
dv.melbay.com/93268

YouTube
www.melbay.com.93268V

WWW.MELBAY.COM

TUNING THE BANJO

The five open strings of the banjo will be of the same pitch as the five notes shown in the illustration of the piano keyboard.

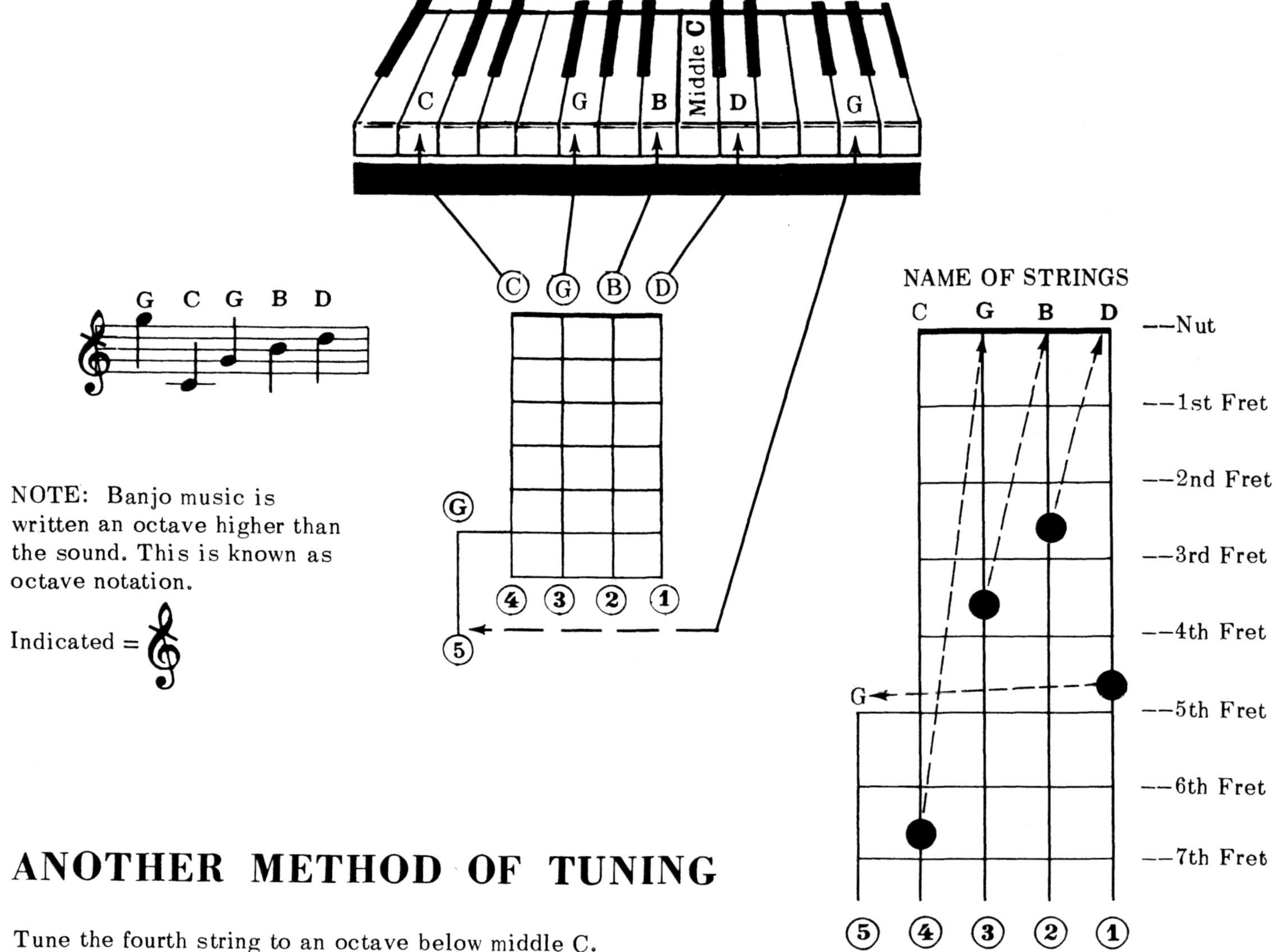

NOTE: Banjo music is written an octave higher than the sound. This is known as octave notation.

Indicated = 𝄞

ANOTHER METHOD OF TUNING

Tune the fourth string to an octave below middle C.

Press the finger behind the 7th-Fret of the C-string and tune the 3rd or G string until it sounds the same pitch as the tone produced on the seventh Fret of the C-String.

Press the finger behind the fourth Fret of the 3rd string and tune the second or B-String until it sounds the same pitch as tone produced.

Press the finger behind the third Fret of the second string and tune the first string until it sounds exactly the same as the tone produced.

The 5th string sounds the same as the tone produced by placing the finger behind the fifth string of the first string.

Electronic Tuners

Electronic tuners are available at your music store. They are a handy device and highly recommended.

The Correct Way To Hold The Banjo

This Is the Pick

Hold it in

this manner ⟶

firmly between the

thumb and first finger.

Use a medium

soft pick.

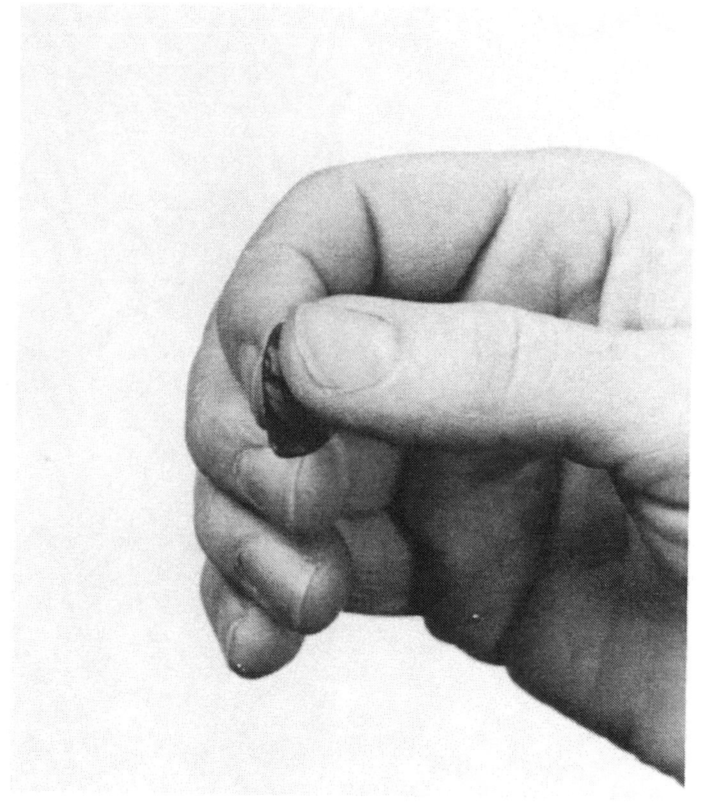

THE LEFT HAND

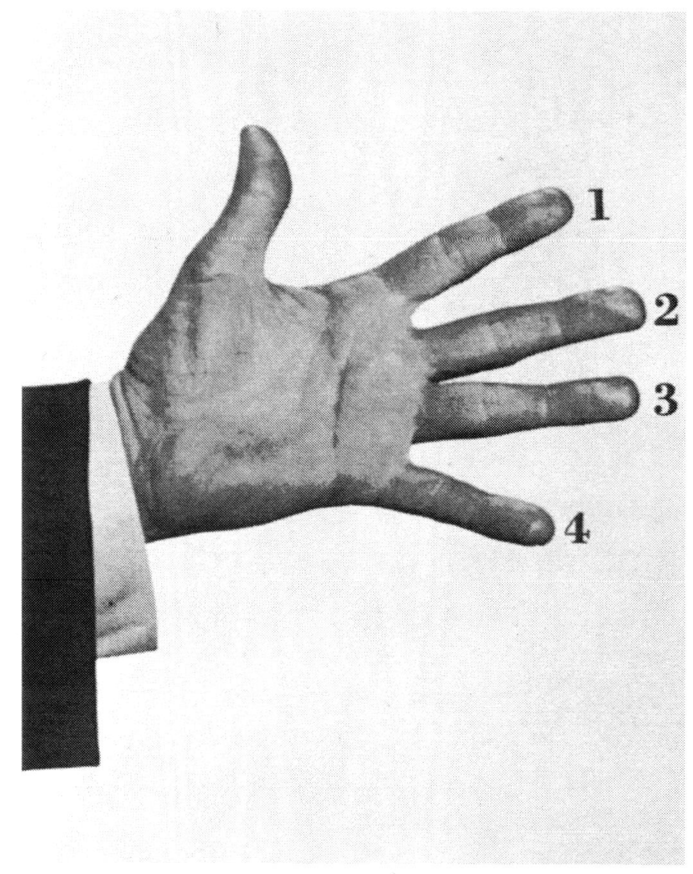

Practice holding the Banjo in this manner.

Keep palm of the hand from the neck of the instrument.

THE FINGERBOARD

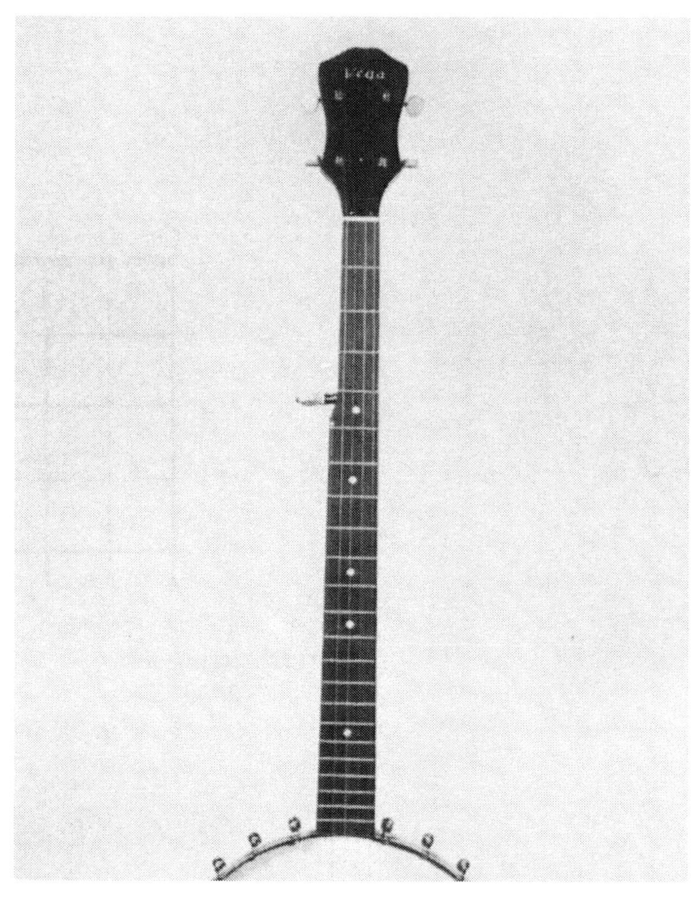

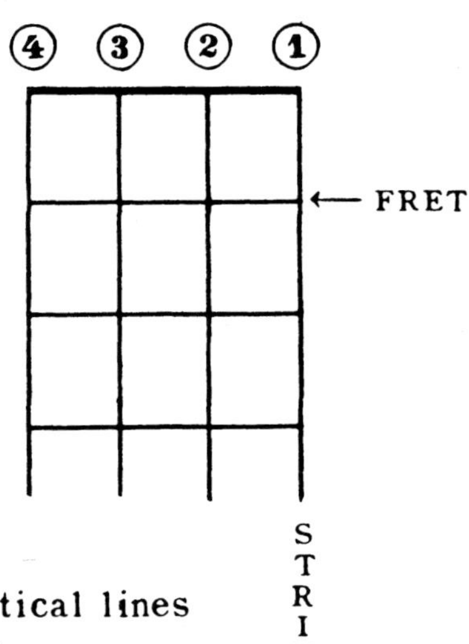

The vertical lines are the strings.

The horizontal lines are the frets.

The encircled numbers are the number of the strings.

= 5th String (open)

Striking the Strings

with the fingers

with the pick

OUR FIRST CHORD

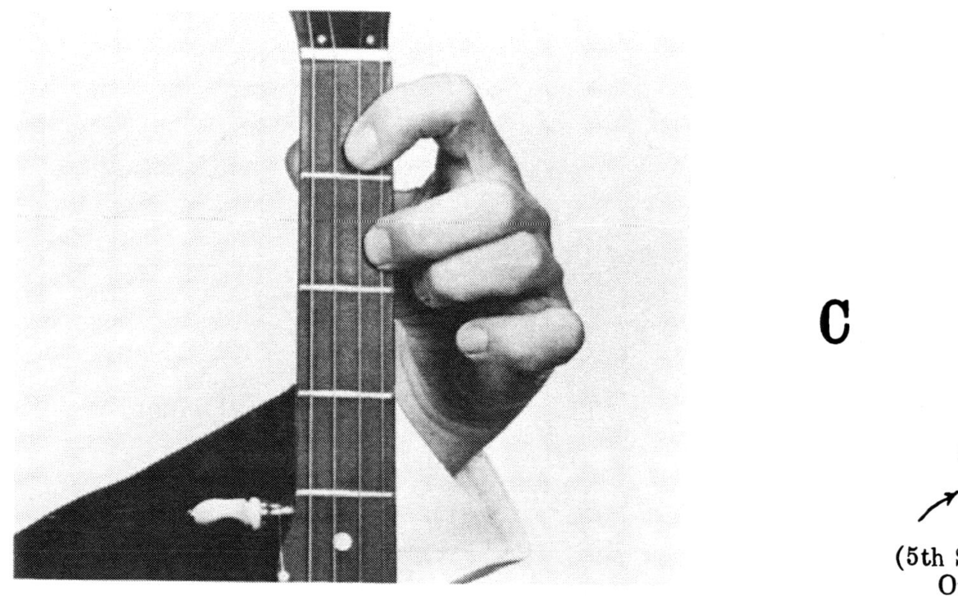

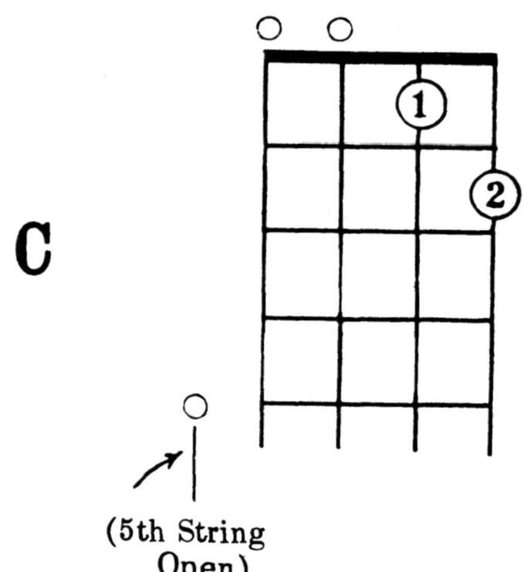

Do not place fingers on the frets but directly behind them.

Do not apply too much pressure.

Practice the above Chord until the tone is clear.

/ / / / = Strokes of the Pick over the Strings.

/// = Strum the C chord three times in succession.

TIME SIGNATURES

$\frac{4}{4}$ or C = COMMON TIME

Hold the C chord and play it in this manner:

C C C C

$\frac{4}{4}$ / / / /   / / / /   / / / /   / / /

$\frac{3}{4}$ = THREE-FOUR or WALTZ TIME

Hold the C chord and play it in the following manner:

C C C C

$\frac{3}{4}$ / / /   / / /   / / /   / / /

$\frac{2}{4}$ = TWO-FOUR TIME

Play it in this manner:

C

$\frac{2}{4}$ / /   / /   / /   / /

THE G7 CHORD

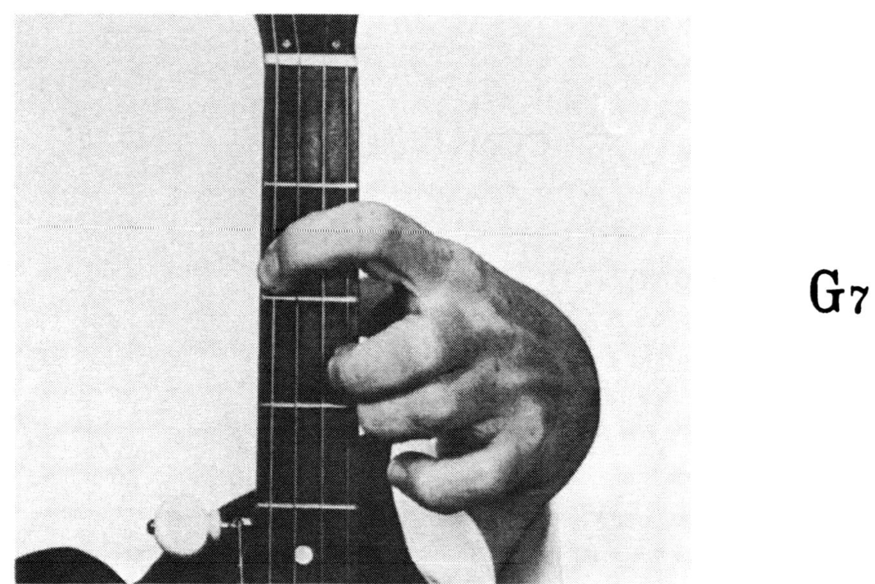

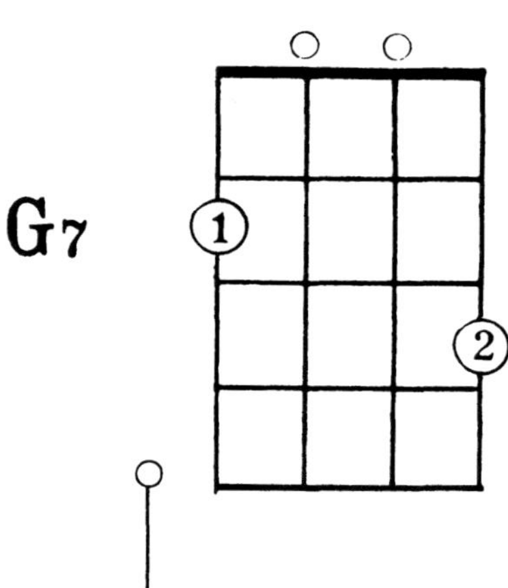

Play the C and G7 chords in the following manner:

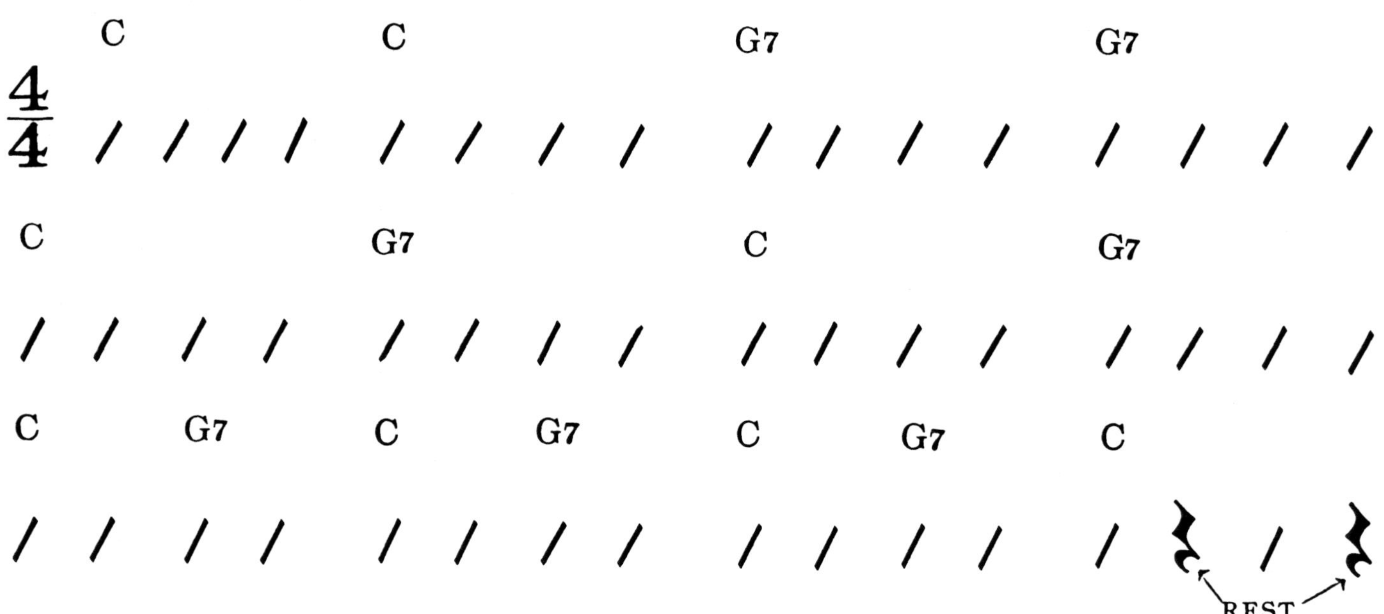

𝄽 = Rest. It indicates a period of silence.

OUR FIRST SONG

(Using the C and G7 Chords)

Long, Long Ago

Be sure to play the chords directly on each word or syllable as indicated.

Down In The Valley

* Continue playing the C chord until you reach the G7 chord.
Play G7 until you arrive at C.

Skip To My Lou

* No chord strokes on words in parenthesis ( ).

Buffalo Gals

Oh, My Darling Clementine

There will be no playing on the pick-up notes at the beginning of the above song.

THE "F" CHORD

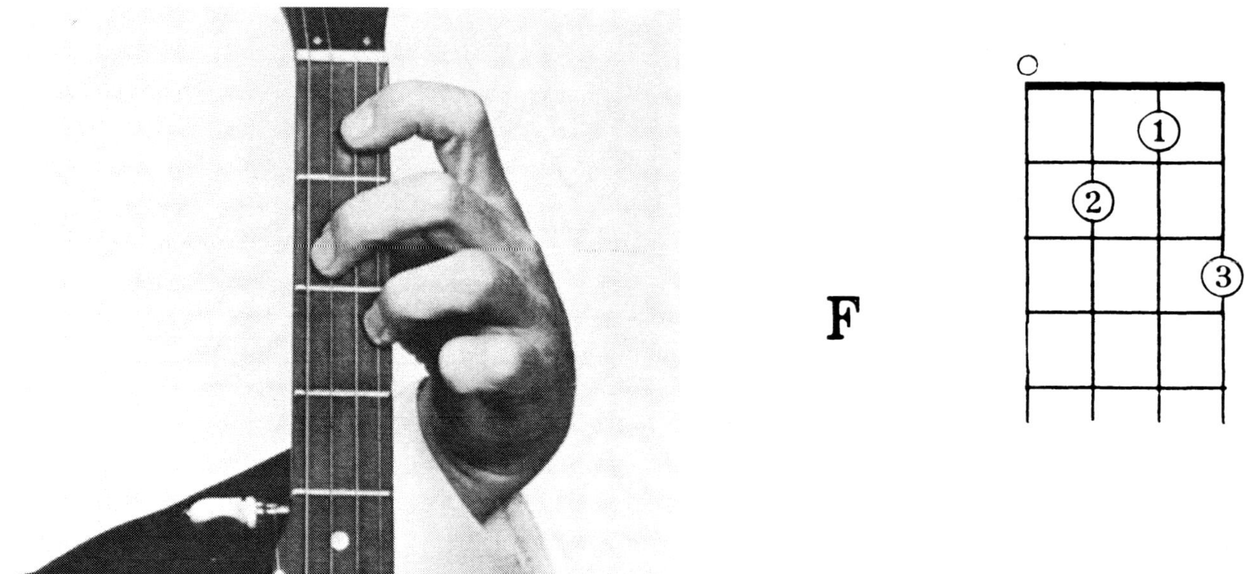

Master the following Chord Study:

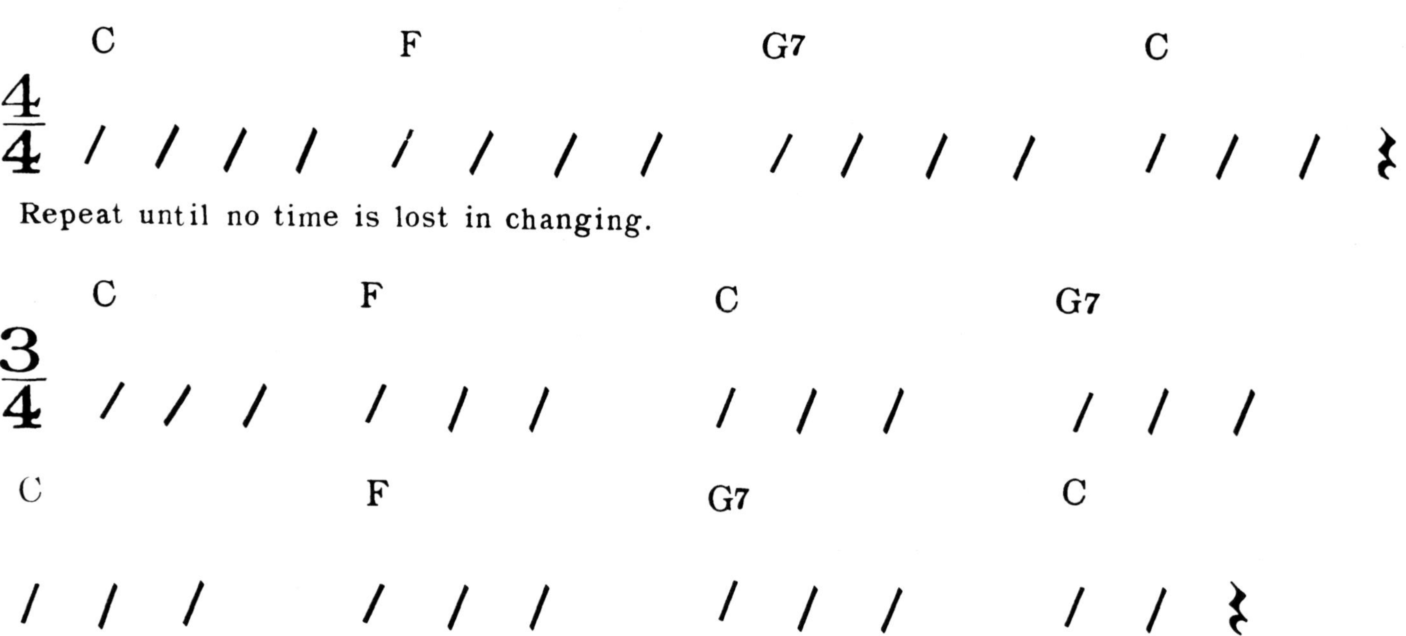

Repeat until no time is lost in changing.

The C, F and G7 chords are the principal chords in the Key of C.

The Blue Tail Fly

* 𝄐 = Hold the note extra long as in a pause.

On Top Of Old Smoky

The Marines Hymn

There Is A Tavern In The Town

* The Pick-up note may be played by striking the third string open.

* Strum the pick over the chord slowly as in a harp style and let it ring.

THE D7 CHORD

Play the following Chord Study:

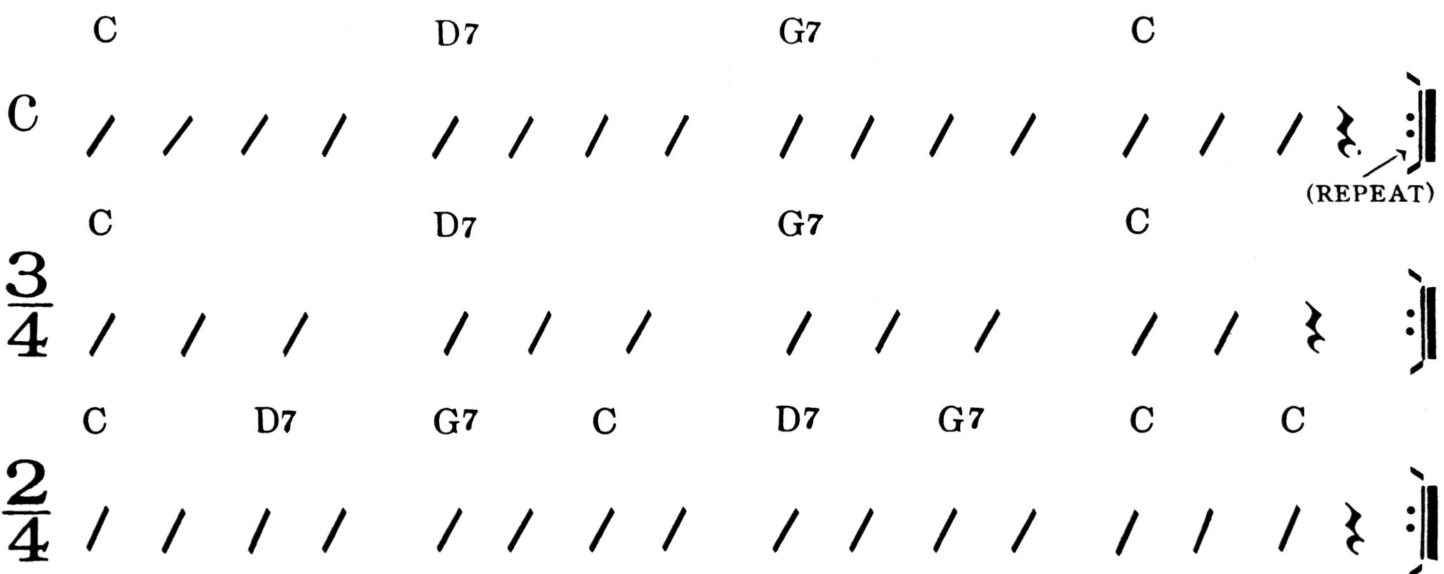

Master the above study before proceeding.

Our Boys Will Shine Tonight

(Introducing the D7 Chord)

In the last measure play the bass note on the first beat, rest and play the C chord on the third beat. The fourth beat is silent.

THE G CHORD

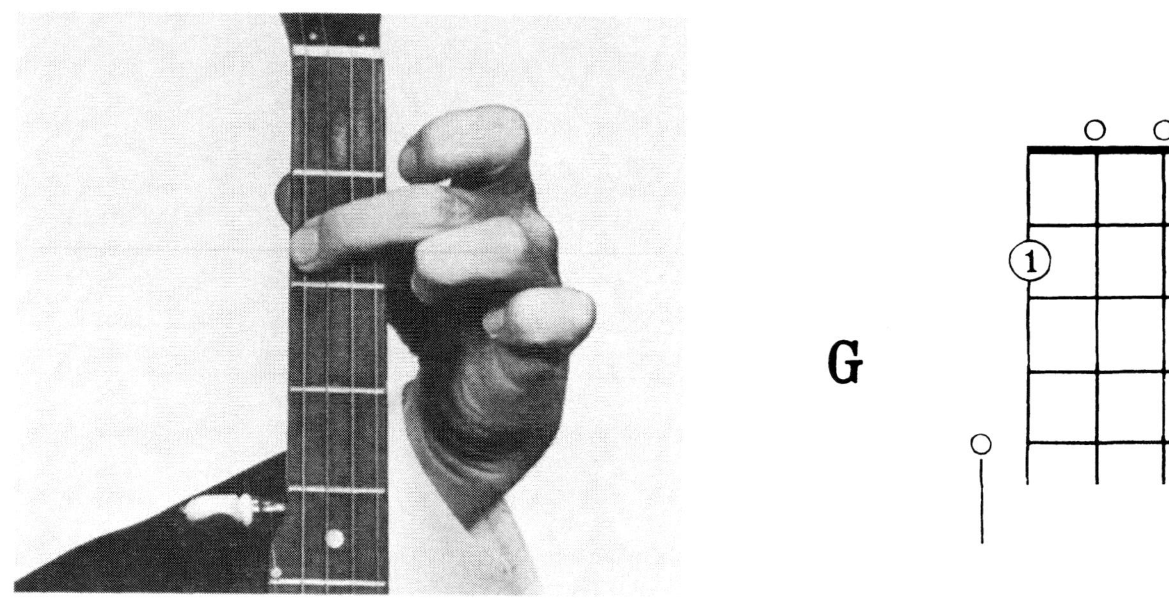

The chords in the Key of G are: G, C and D7.

Play the following Chord Study:

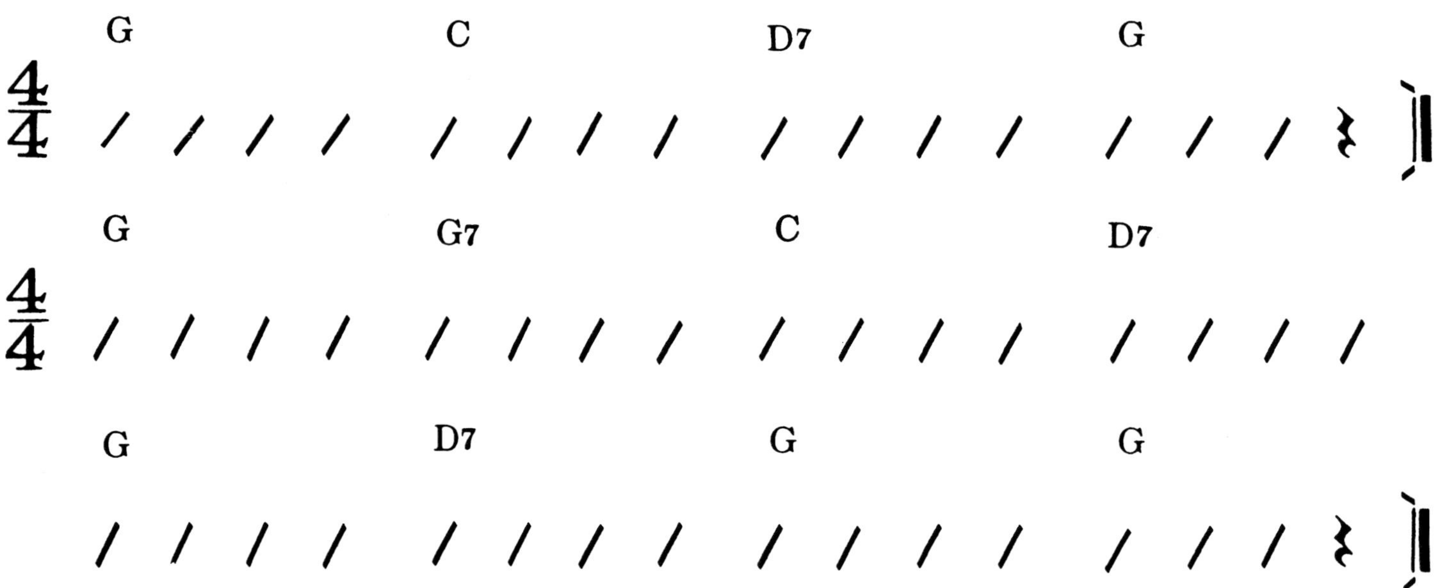

The Old Grey Mare

She'll Be Coming Round The Mountain

Hand Me Down My Walking Cane

In order to start your song in the correct key, strum the principal chord lightly before beginning. In the above song the principal or tonic chord is G.

Red River Valley

SOME MORE CHORDS

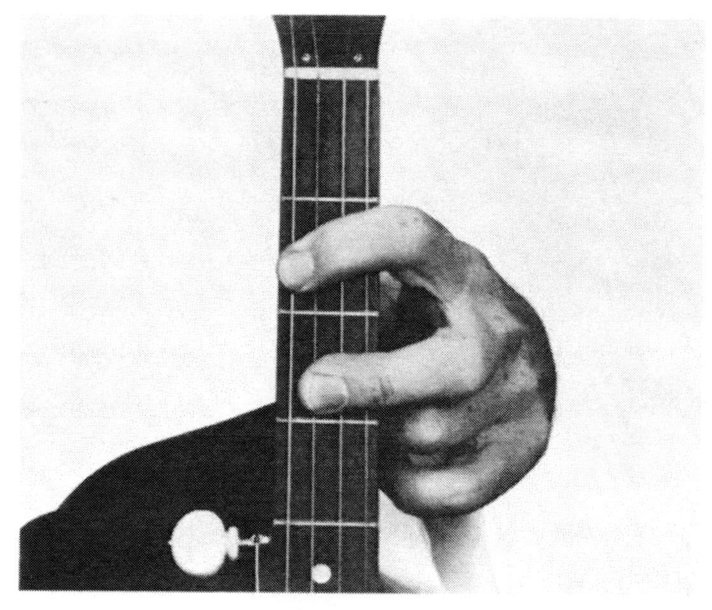

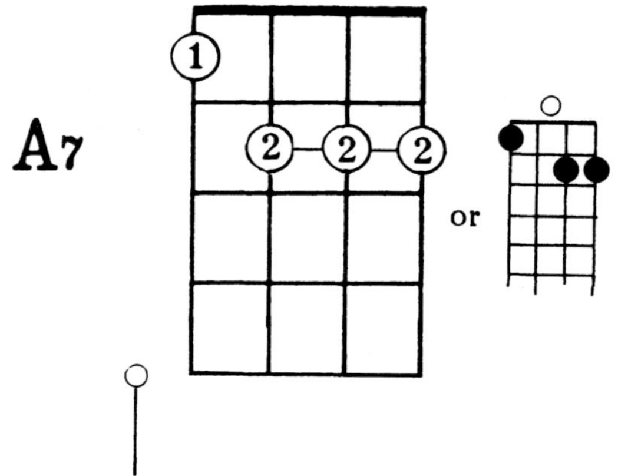

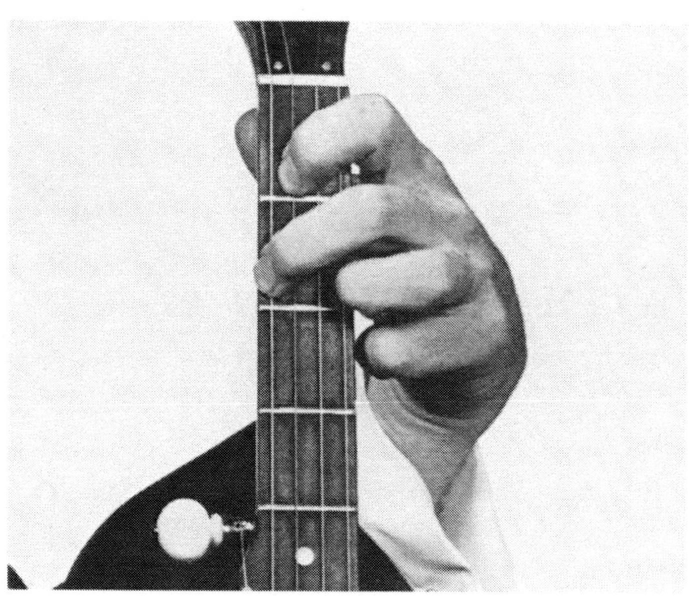

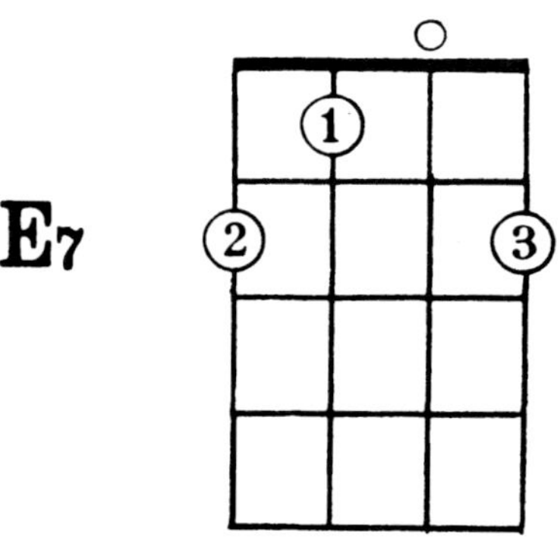

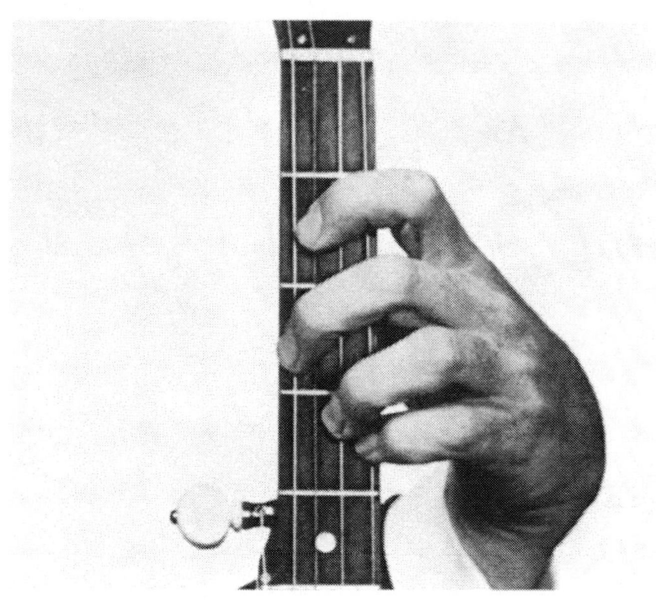

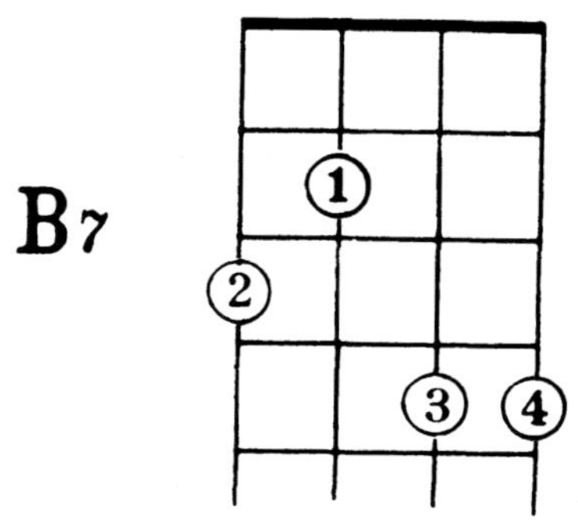

FUN WITH CHORDS IN "C"

3/4

C	E7	A7	D7	G7	C
/ / /	/ / /	/ / /	/ / /	/ / /	/ / 𝄽

4/4

C	E7	A7	D7	G7	C
/ / / /	/ / / /	/ / / /	/ / / /	/ / / /	/ 𝄽 / 𝄽

MORE FUN WITH CHORDS IN "G"

3/4

G	B7	E7	A7	D7	G
/ / /	/ / /	/ / /	/ / /	/ / /	/ / 𝄽

4/4

G	B7	E7	A7	D7	G
/ / / /	/ / / /	/ / / /	/ / / /	/ / / /	/ / / 𝄽

Home on The Range

I've Been Working On The Railroad

G G G
Some (one's) in the kitch-(en) with Di – nah – some (one's) in (the) kitch(en) I
D7 G C
know - o - o - o Some-(one's) in the kitch-(en) with Di – nah –
G D7 G G G
strum(min') on (the) old ban - jo – – Fee – fi – fid-(lee) i - o –
G D7 G
fee - fi - fid - (lee) - i - o - o - o - o Fee – fi –
C G D7 G
fid-(lee) - i - o – strum(min') on the old ban - jo. – –

In The Evening By The Moonlight

In the above song
strum the chords slowly.

THE D CHORD

D

1
1
2
3

D G A7 D
4/4 / / / / / / / / / / / / / / / /
D G A7 D
3/4 / / / / / / / / / / / 𝄽
D B7 E7 A7
4/4 / / / / / / / / / / / / / / / /
D D7 G D
/ / / / / / / / / / / / / / / 𝄽

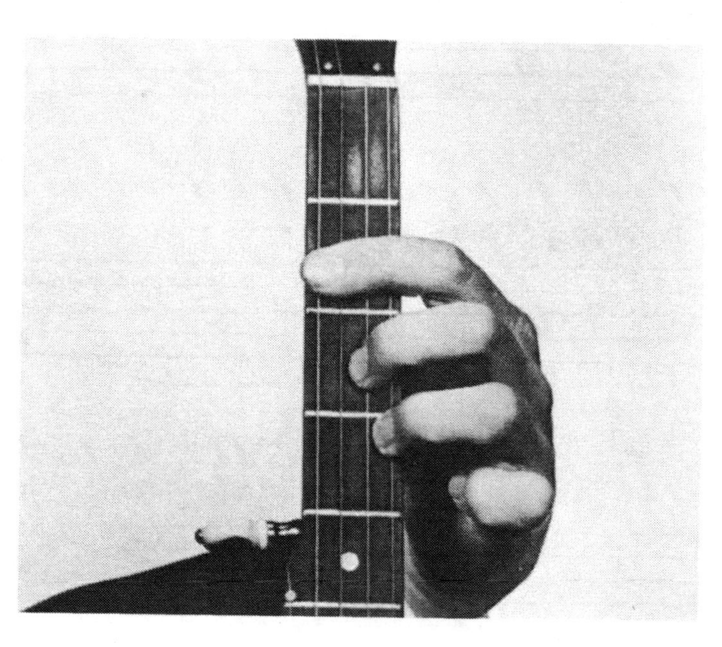

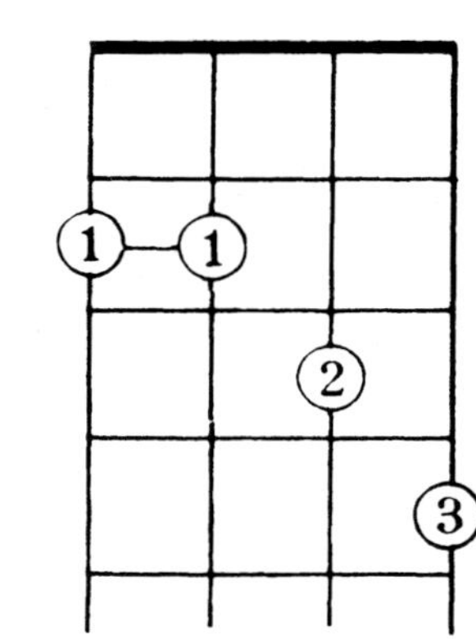

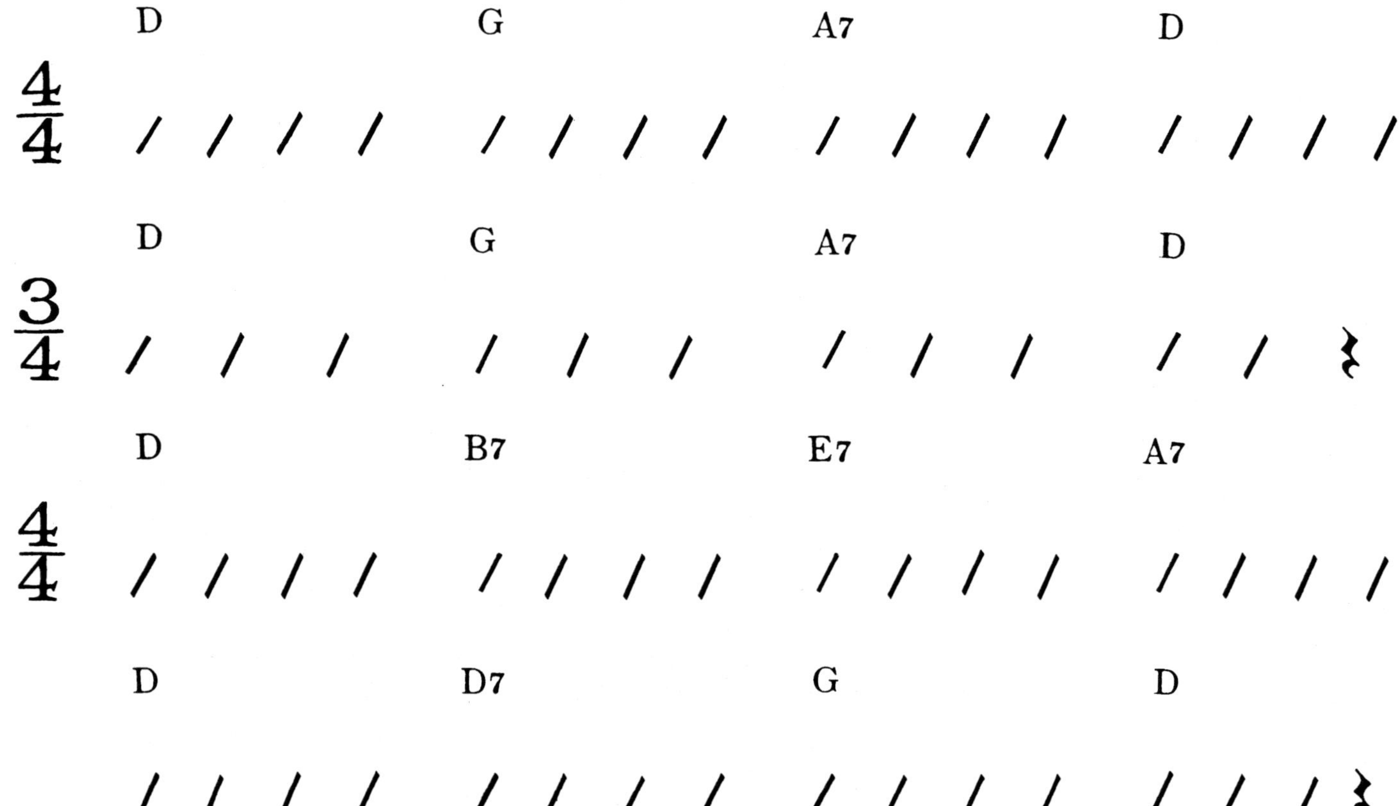

Darling Nellie Gray

My Bonnie

D G D D
My Bon-nie lies o - ver the o - cean My Bon-nie lies
E7 A7 D G D
o-ver the sea My Bon-nie lies o -ver the o - cean
D E7 A7 D
Oh bring back my Bon-nie to me.
CHORUS
D E7 A7
Bring back, Bring back, Bring back my
A7 D D E7
Bon-nie to me, to me Bring back, Bring
E7 A7 D
back Oh bring back my Bon-nie to me.

Little Annie Rooney

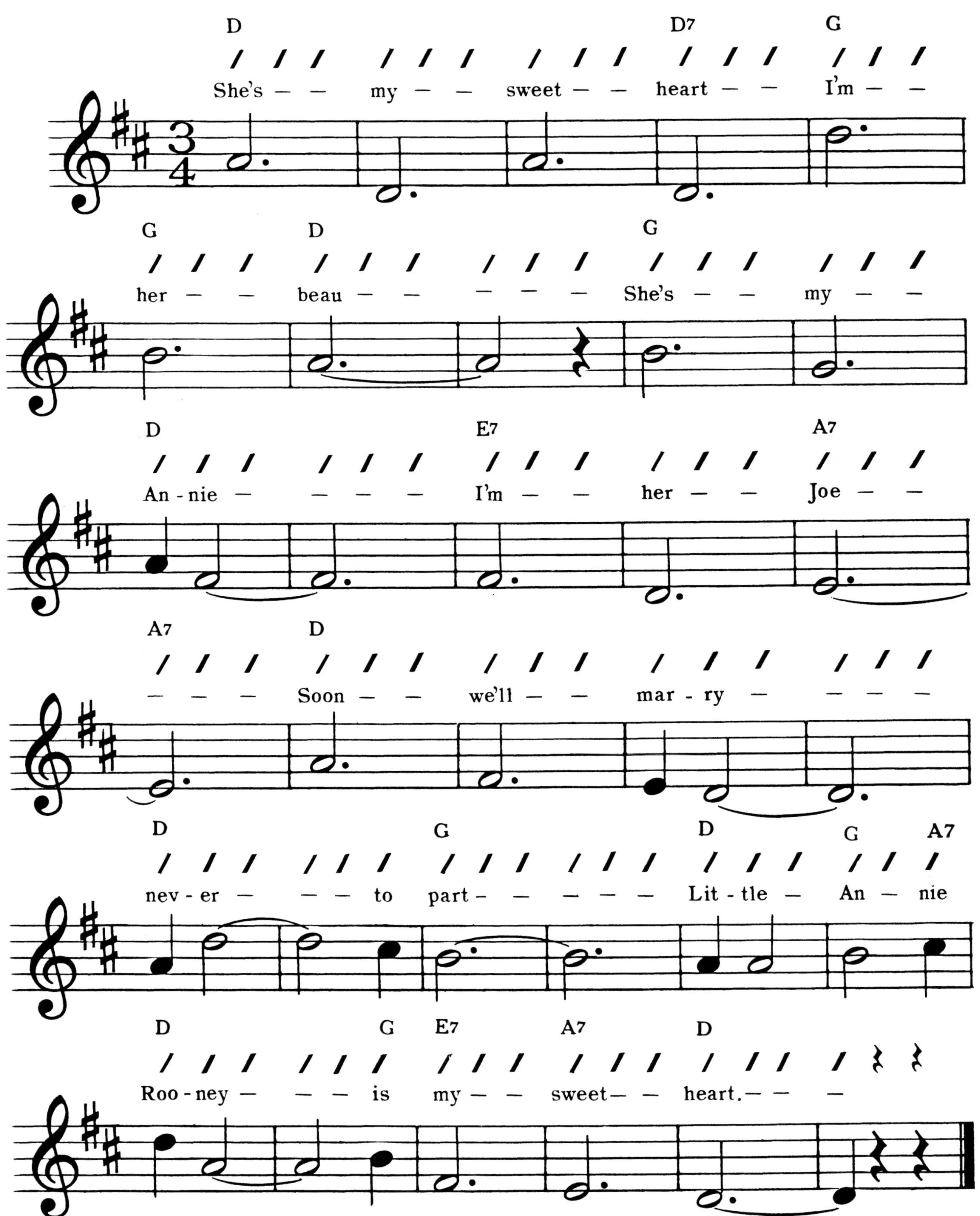

Oh! Susanna

D A7 D
I come from Al-a-bam-a with my ban-jo on my knee I'm g'wan to Lou-si-
D D A7 D
an - a my true love for to see It rained all night the day I left, the
A7 D D A7 D
weath-er it was dry The sun so hot I froze to death Su-san-na don't you cry.
G D A7 D
Oh Su - san-na Oh don't you cry for me I've come from Al - a -
D D A7 D G D
bam-a with my ban-jo on my knee Oh Su-san-na Oh don't you cry for
A7 D D A7 D
me I've come from Al-a-bam-a with my ban-jo on my knee.

Good Night Ladies

SUMMARY

The Major Chords

Each Form must be thoroughly mastered before proceeding to the next.

I

Frets	1	2	3	4	5	6	7	8	9	10	11	12	13
Chords	F	F# Gb	G	Ab	A	Bb	B	C	Db C#	D	Eb	E	F

III

Frets	1	2	3	4	5	6	7	8	9	10	11	12	13
Chords	Db C#	D	Eb	E	F	Gb F#	G	Ab	A	Bb	B	C	Db C#

V

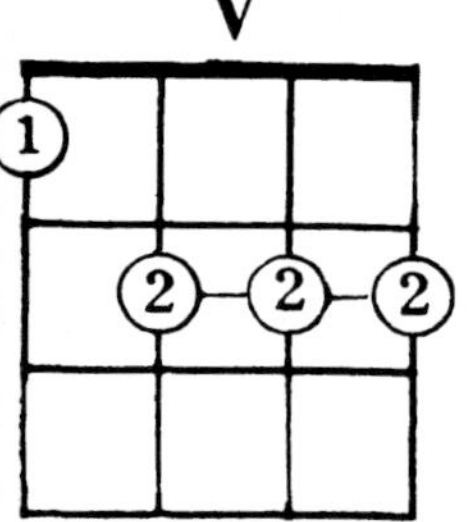

Frets	1	2	3	4	5	6	7	8	9	10	11	12	13
Chords	A	Bb	B	C	Db C#	D	Eb	E	F	Gb F#	G	Ab	A

The Minor Chords

Im

Frets	1	2	3	4	5	6	7	8	9	10	11	12	13
Chords	Fm	Gbm F#m	Gm	Abm	Am	Bbm	Bm	Cm	Dbm C#m	Dm	Ebm	Em	Fm

IIIm

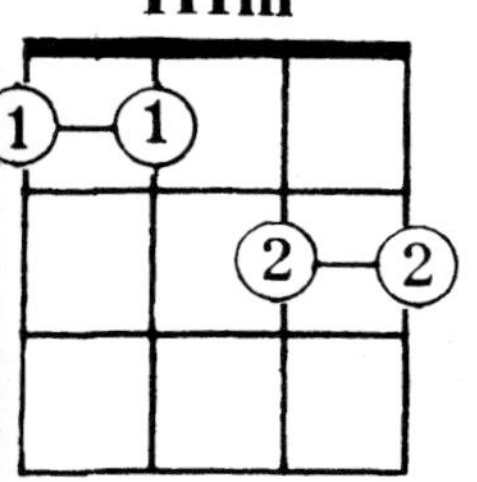

Frets	1	2	3	4	5	6	7	8	9	10	11	12	13
Chords	Dbm C#m	Dm	Ebm	Em	Fm	Gbm F#m	Gm	Abm	Am	Bbm	Bm	Cm	Dbm C#m

Vm

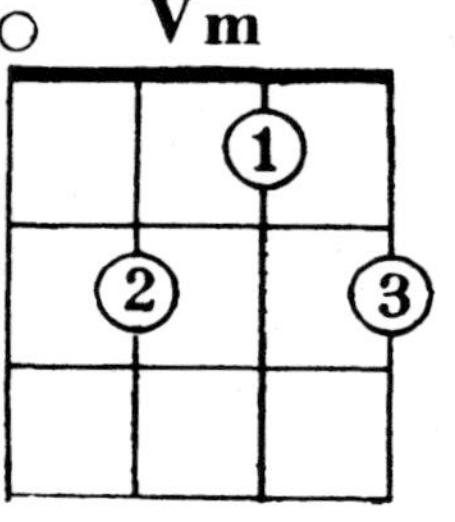

Frets	1	2	3	4	5	6	7	8	9	10	11	12	13
Chords	Am	Bbm	Bm	C	Dbm C#m	Dm	Ebm	Em	Fm	Gbm F#m	Gm	Abm	Am

THE SEVENTH CHORDS

I7

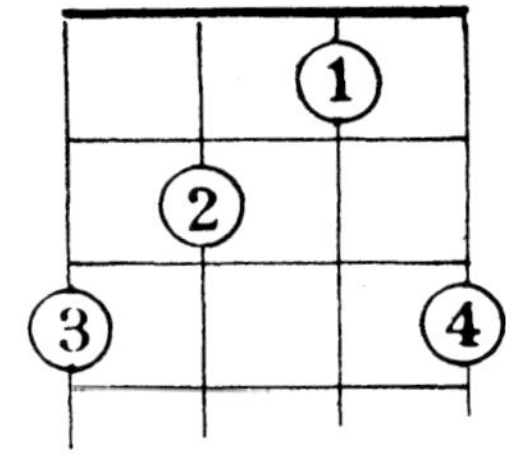

Frets	1	2	3	4	5	6	7	8	9	10	11	12
Chords	F7	Gb7 F#7	G7	Ab7	A7	Bb7	B7	C7	Db7 C#7	D7	Eb7	E7

III7

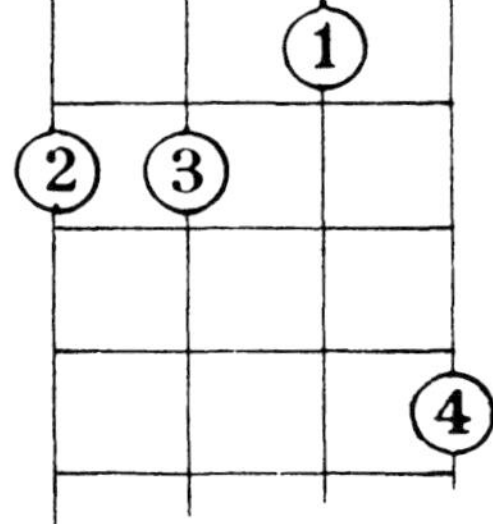

Frets	1	2	3	4	5	6	7	8	9	10	11	12
Chords	D7	Eb7	E7	F7	Gb7 F#7	G7	Ab7	A7	Bb7	B7	C7	Db7 C#7

V7

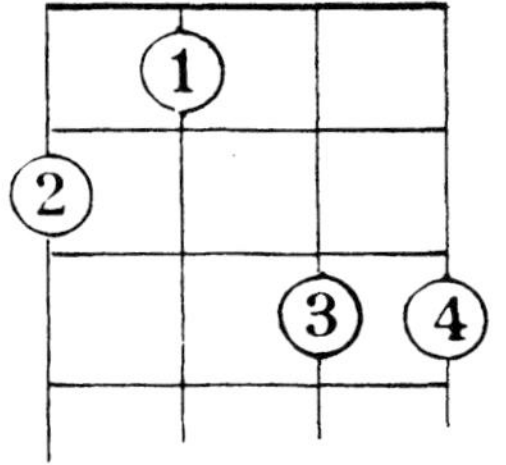

Frets	1	2	3	4	5	6	7	8	9	10	11	12
Chords	Bb7	B7	C7	Db7 C#7	D7	Eb7	E7	F7	Gb7 F#7	G7	Ab7	A7

VII7

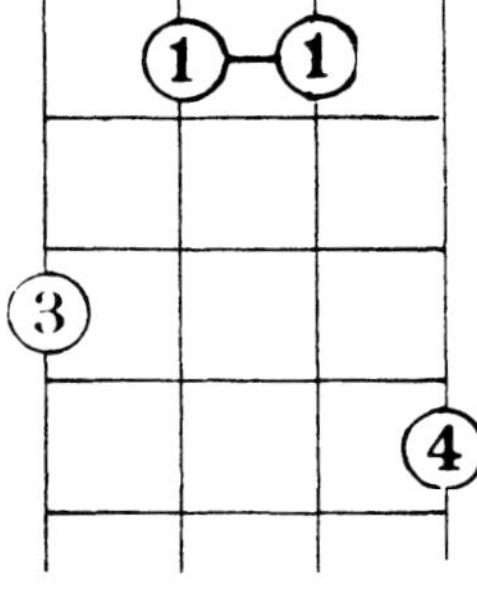

Frets	1	2	3	4	5	6	7	8	9	10	11	12
Chords	Ab7	A7	Bb7	B7	C7	Db7 C#7	D7	Eb7	E7	F7	Gb7 F#7	G7